My Path to Happy

Struggles with my mental health and all the wonderful things that happened after...

SIMON &
SCHUSTER

London · New York · Sydney · Toronto · New Delhi

A CBS COMPANY

Written and illustrated by Charlotte Reed

First published in Great Britain by Simon & Schuster UK Ltd, 2019
A CBS COMPANY

1 3 5 7 9 10 8 6 4 2

Simon & Schuster UK Ltd
1st Floor
222 Gray's Inn Road
London WC1X 8HB

www.simonandschuster.co.uk
www.simonandschuster.com.au
www.simonandschuster.co.in

Simon & Schuster Australia, Sydney
Simon & Schuster India, New Delhi

The author and publishers have made all reasonable efforts to contact copyright-holders
for permission, and apologise for any omissions or errors in the form of credits given.
Corrections may be made to future printings.

A CIP catalogue record for this book is available from the British Library

Hardback ISBN: 978-1-4711-7971-6
eBook ISBN: 978-1-4711-7972-3

Printed in China

Important Note
This book is not intended as a substitute for medical advice or
treatment. Any person with a condition requiring medical attention
should consult a qualified medical practitioner or qualified therapist

This book is dedicated to my sister, Kate, and my brother, Richard, who are quite simply the world's best lighthouses.

Hello, I'm Charlotte Reed and I'd like to tell you a story. It's about something that happened to me. It's a sad story but thankfully it has a really positive and happy ending.

The *reason* I want to share it is in case it can *help* you.

You see, we all experience difficulties in life, and we all need a little *support* as we go through them. Maybe my story will give you *hope* that your tough time can turn around for the ♥better,♥ just like mine did...

SO LET'S BEGIN!!

Once upon a time, I became very depressed. I hadn't been feeling that happy for a while but I suddenly started feeling a lot worse. I was 30 years old and I was living and working in London.

Unfortunately, the depression lasted for over two years. At first I struggled daily with panic attacks, anxiety and an incredibly low mood. The anxiety made me feel like I was being chased by an axe murderer!

Whereas the low mood could only be described as 'gut-wrenching sorrow' - the kind of intense grief and pain you'd feel if someone you loved very dearly had just died.

Suddenly the world felt alien to me. I had absolutely <u>no</u> idea what was happening.

My depressed state was also accompanied by physical symptoms. I had terrible daily headaches, and this really strange sensation that a torrent of water was gushing through my head. My vision was also affected. When I looked through my eyes nothing seemed real any more, like I was in a waking dream. It was as though I was disconnected from reality and observing life from behind a thick pane of glass. Everyone and everything looked two-dimensional instead of three-dimensional.

Life feels like I'm looking at a photograph of it, rather than it being real!

My whole body also felt completely hollow and floaty, like I was a ghost and not made of solid matter. The sensation was so overwhelming I started questioning whether I was indeed a ghost!

After two weeks of feeling that way I went to see my GP and told him all my symptoms. He immediately diagnosed me with depression and anxiety and recommended I go on anti-depressants. However, he looked quite puzzled when I said I felt like I was a ghost and not really here!

I just don't feel real doctor!

erm... ok... that's unusual.

I knew in my heart I didn't want to take medication so my GP suggested counselling instead. Unfortunately, for me personally, it didn't really help. The counsellor wanted me to tell her how I felt, whereas I just needed reassurance I wasn't going mad.

Counsellor lady →

So, tell me how you feel.

OK, I feel an aching sadness to my core, anxiety so intense it's as though I'm being constantly strangled, and my body feels totally hollow, like I'm floating around in space!

After a few sessions of counselling with no improvement, I realised I'd have to dig deeper to get to the bottom of my mind's strange goings on.

Luckily, the psychiatrist was able to explain the symptoms that my doctor couldn't.

As well as having depression and anxiety you have a condition called depersonalisation disorder. It's an altered mental state that can be triggered by trauma, stress or recreational drug use, and it makes the sufferer feel like they are dreaming reality instead of being present living it. It is incredibly disturbing to experience but it can gradually fade over time. I therefore recommend you take anti-depressants to at least tackle the depression you feel.

I told the psychiatrist I needed time to think.
s I walked home I felt so alone — although it
as good to have a name for the unreal feeling that
'd been experiencing, it sounded like there wasn't a
uick and easy 'magic cure.' As for the anxiety and
depression, well, yes, I could take medication for
those, but my heart still didn't feel it was the
right choice for me.

I just don't
know if I
want to take
something
chemical...

I felt the best thing to do was wait a while, to see if the depression and anxiety would somehow go away on their own. Unfortunately, however, things only got worse.

I suddenly didn't feel able to do basic physical things. Even taking a shower became a huge, scary event and, as such, often didn't happen!

I slowly started to be able to function less and less. Everything felt like a huge, impossible task. I'd lie in bed for hours on end, my thoughts racing uncontrollably. I would sometimes hyperventilate and tears would pour down my cheeks and collect on my pillow. My brain just wasn't operating right — everything felt like it was in the wrong order and nothing made sense any more. I really did think, 'This is it, I'm losing my mind, I'm losing touch with reality.'

It was the most frightening and unfamiliar feeling I've ever experienced in my whole life...

By that point my thoughts had spiralled so badly out of control that I felt totally desperate. So much so that I started to believe the only option I had was to end my life. I really didn't want to die, but I just couldn't work out how to live any more in my current state. So I did what anyone should do in that situation — I called someone.

That Someone was my older brother Richard. He also lived in London and immediately said I should go and stay with him.

I couldn't go to work for a while
and spent most of my days staring up
at the ceiling of my brother's spare room,
asking myself strange questions:

- who am I?
- What am I?
- what is the point of
  human existence?

grapes

Richard had to go to work during the day but he'd call to check on me and spend time with me in the evenings to keep me company.

Some days I'd try to _force_ myself to do normal, simple things but even the thought of going to buy a pint of milk felt paralysing.

We need milk so that means: finding some loose change, locating my shoes, walking to the shop, speaking to the shop keeper. Garh! It's all too much!

It is safe to say it was an incredibly frightening and traumatic time, and I can't thank my brother enough for the support he gave me. At that point I hadn't told my parents what was going on as I didn't want to worry them, but I did confide in my older sister, Kate, who was an absolute lifeline to me. I can honestly say that Kate walked every single step of my mental health journey with me she was my companion during the dark night of my soul. She lived on a farm in the Lake District a few hundred miles away but she was, without exception, ♥ <u>always</u> ♥ at the end of the phone whenever I needed her. And I needed her <u>a lot</u>!!

Every day I phoned her 3 or 4 times, barely able to breathe because my anxiety was so bad. She had 3 small children but never once did she make me feel that she was too busy to talk.

Whenever I was caught in a full-blown panic attack, Kate suggested something that really helped. It was to be in nature, even if that was just in the park at the end of my brother's street. sh told me to feel the earth beneath my feet, or to lie on the grass. She suggested I focus my attention on a tree blowing in the wind and to even hold on to the tree for support while I wa hyperventilating. All her suggestions were to try to ground me, bring me back into my body and allow the healing effects of nature to slowly reduce my anxiety. Doing these things meant I felt a bit safer while my world was spinning out of control.

I actually believe the love and support my brother and sister gave me during this time were the only things keeping me going. Knowing they were there made me feel less alone. They truly were my lighthouse in my emotional storm.

And so life carried on as it had. I was back at work by that stage but, because I was still struggling, I'd continued to stay at my brother's house. Then one evening, staring at the ceiling of my brother's spare room brought me sudden insight...

my sister Kate agreed...

There are loads of alternative things you could try - things like acupuncture and nutritional therapy, for example.

yes! Both brilliant ideas!

And just like that, my road to recovery began... with Kate there every step of the way.

The first thing I did was to arrange an appointment with my sister's friend Wendy, an acupuncturist based in London. When I got to her clinic I broke down in tears - I told her everything; about the intense sorrow, the panic attacks, the anxiety and the depersonalisation disorder. Wendy just listened and when I finally finished she calmly said,

Don't worry, I can help you.

A wave of relief rushed over me. <u>Finally</u> there might be a solution! Wendy went on to say,

Come for a treatment once a week and we'll get to the bottom of this. Also, Charlotte, I know your struggle seems terrible but I have a feeling that one day you're going to use it to help other people.

At the time I was feeling so ill that it was hard to believe her— but a tiny part of me suddenly sprung alive with hope. the thought that one day there might be a purpose to my pain gave me renewed strength.

I had acupuncture once a week for quite a few months. I found Wendy's treatments to be incredibly therapeutic; the combination of the needle and her talking to me really helped me make sense of what was going on and I gradually stopped feeling so anxious.

I also visited a nutritionist to be tested for any vitamin and mineral deficiencies, and under her guidance, I started taking supplements to address any imbalances. I also changed my diet to include really healthy and nutritious foods like:

Brown rice   oily fish   fruit   veg   good fats

I learned that making sure your diet is as good as it can be can really make a difference to your mental health.

Exercise also formed a big part of my recovery. I started power-walking round the streets of London for at least 1.5 hours every, single day. This really helped get my endorphins going.

A few months ago I was a greasy, terrified mess and couldn't get out of bed. Now I'm able to enjoy a long walk every day! Although this achievement is small, it's a sign I'm heading in the right direction. I will therefore take note of every small achievement I make to remind myself I'm getting better.

Happiness

Another idea I had was to make myself think of one positive thought each morning to try to coax my brain into thinking more optimistically. I won't lie, it was virtually impossible to do it, but I forced myself, and even posted the thought as my Facebook status. Because my friends started to expect my 'Thought of The Day', it meant I had a responsibility to them, as well as myself, to do it. Soon my 'Thought of The day' became really popular and, over time, friends started to ask if I'd turn my thoughts into a book! I loved the idea, but I still didn't feel well enough, or have enough confidence to do it... so I politely declined.

And so two years slowly passed, and with the weekly acupuncture, the vitamin supplements, the change in diet, the daily exercise and the daily positive thoughts I was writing I eventually did make a full recovery from the depression and anxiety. It had kind of been a 'two steps forward, one step back' journey. Some days were better than others but slowly the depressed and anxious feelings dissipated. As for the depersonalisation disorder and its weird dreamlike sensation, unfortunately that still remained. I discovered that, while many sufferers do eventually recover, for some the condition persists... and I seemed to be one of them! It was deeply frustrating but because there was nothing I could do about it, over time I learnt to live with it, and make peace with it.

That 'good' feeling lasted a few weeks, but then, without any warning whatsoever, another challenge suddenly presented itself in my life; very soon after recovering from the depression and anxiety I began to experience problems on a physical level.

I was working as a legal secretary at the time and suddenly developed repetitive strain injury from using a computer keyboard. The RSI had affected my nervous system and meant I was in constant pain. I didn't know what to do. The doctor's prognosis wasn't good either.

Suddenly I found myself signed off work and on sick pay. My days were filled with seeing various specialists and doing physio to try to help my body heal.

Urrgh! Nerve pain feels like electric shocks shooting through me, evil ants crawling over my skin and biting me, and my muscles ache so much even turning a door handle hurts!

Door of Doom

This period of my life was not all bad, however. By chance I happened to meet a lovely man called Johnny Lucas, a talented musician with scruffy hair and a beautiful, warm heart. We instantly fell in love.

Will you be my girlfriend?

Totally! 100%. Yes!!

ROCK

← Soul mates →

Johnny had the lovely idea of writing songs together to keep my mind off my pain. He wrote the music and I wrote the lyrics. Being creative was so much fun and I really think it prevented the depression from setting in again.

And not just that, his love also acted like a healing balm on my aching body and soul, and over time I eventually did get better. At that point I feared returning to my job in case the RSI came back, so I realised I needed to find a career that no longer involved computer work. I'd still been writing my daily positive thoughts all that time and friends pleaded with me _again_ to turn them into a book.

Write your book!

DO IT!

And this time I finally listened, realising I could write the entire thing by hand!

I was extremely nervous about doing it, but Johnny w so supportive and encouraging I took the leap of faith needed to resign from my job in the Corporat world to become an author. I only had enough money saved to support me for three months, but a little voice inside told me somehow everything would be ok!

Every day I sat at my dining room table hand-writing my book. I decided to draw a little cartoon character on each page saying one of my positive thoughts in a speech bubble, characters like:

<u>The Professor of Truth</u>

Contrary to popular belief, being hard on yourself will not make you strong, but being kind to yourself <u>WILL</u>.

and... <u>The Snail</u>

Nobody said modern-day life had to be busy or stressful. The pace you go is up to you.

And other characters like:

Betty

you will never live your heart's desires or create an authentic life as long as you comply with living someone else's dreams.

Clever cat

Don't try to be better than everyone else, just try to be better at being yourself.

One of the Characters, the Shoeless Guru, seemed to be the wisest of them all, and as I drew him, it was almost like he came alive on the page to communicate his wisdom directly to me...!

The more days I spent writing and drawing, the more the other characters would also come alive on the page to speak their wisdom to me too...

The
Happy
Hippy →

Charlotte, I'm here to tell you that life only changes because your soul is ready for a change.

You're so right, Happy Hippy! And even if that change is difficult it always bring growth.

It was a really magical experience and I became completely engrossed in the world of the characters I was creating. Suddenly I felt like I had all these lovely companions and guides who were looking out for me.

At that point I still didn't know what to call my book - but then a sudden 'Open Sesame!' style voice appeared in my head and boomed at me 'You should call it "May The Thought Be With You".' I thought it was just PERFECT! And so, the world of 'May The Thoughts Be With You' and all its little characters was born. When the book was actually ready, however, all the publishers turned it down. I was disappointed, but the Professor of Truth soon appeared to help.

I know it's a setback but do not be defeated! You should self-publish instead! If you can get through 2 years of depression and anxiety, and also learn to live with depersonalisation disorder, you can certainly work out how to sell a book...!

You're so right! That's what I will do!

The next day I took my savings and got some copies of 'May The Thoughts Be With You' printed. I then walked around London with my rucksack full of books asking in independent book shops if they'd take it.

Excuse me, sir, would you like to stock my book?

Hmm... OK! Let me try 10 copies.

The Notting Hill Bookshop

Yes! The famous bookshop from the film 'Notting Hill' was the first shop of many to start selling my book.

Within a few weeks I managed to get my book stocked in lots of shops. The response was incredible. Customers liked it so much the shops would sell out almost immediately and I had to keep delivering more books in a large suitcase! Johnny Lucas also kindly built me an online shop — of course I still couldn't use a computer so I ran my entire business from my iPhone.

...ife was going marvellously. Then Betty, one of my favourite characters, appeared with a brilliant idea

Your book is selling so well in shops and online, why don't you take a stall at Portobello Road Market in Notting Hill and sell it there too?!

So that's what I did...!

Local Artist

Roll up, roll up! Get your positive thoughts here!

And that's when everything _really_ took off! A customer would buy a book then return an hour later saying they wanted copies for everyone they knew. It seemed like everyone loved the positive thoughts and little cartoon characters, and I sold thousands of copies in a very short time. People then started to follow 'May The Thoughts Be With You' on facebook and would come from all over the world to my stall to ge a signed copy.

Korea

Spain

France

China

Hong Kong

oz

my goodnes look at the queue!

Even famous actors, popstars and well-known MPs heard about my thriving book stall and decided to pay me a visit. I couldn't believe it! And then, I almost fainted when one day a king arrived. He was surrounded by body guards as he made his way to my stall. It was like a scene out of a movie!

It was all so overwhelming. I couldn't believe that my little book, which had originated from such a dark, sad and lonely time, was now being appreciated and enjoyed by so many people. It seemed like Wendy, my acupuncturist, had been right when she'd said my suffering and experience would help other people. I'd get email after email from customers thanking me for writing the book. One person's feedback stood out in particular — a lady wrote to me to say she had suicidal depression but my book had given her hope that she could recover, just like I had. Her email was so moving it made me cry! And just when I thought I couldn't get any more emotional, something happened that took me by total surprise. A publisher heard about my book and contacted me to offer me a global book publishing deal!

I was so excited to sign it. Not only was it a wonderful validation of all my hard work, but it also meant my book would now be able to reach and help even more people. When 'May The Thoughts Be With You' was released round the world I suddenly found myself being asked to appear on TV and radio to speak about depression...

Wargh! Look! Our creator's on the telly!

BBC Newsnight

Hi, I'm Charlotte. I want to spread awareness of mental health and help reduce the stigma associated with it.

I even got given a weekly 'positive thinking' column in a national newspaper. Life couldn't have been better; my book got translated into lots of different languages and Johnny and I moved into a new home together. I was <u>so</u> happy!

Love nest

Here's to the next chapter of our lives together Johnny!

But that's the thing about life — it's so unpredictable and can turn upside down in a heartbeat. And sadly, that is EXACTLY what it did...

Bizarrely, the new home Johnny and I had moved into started to make me feel very strange. I began itching, coughing, sneezing and found it hard to breathe. I got headaches, sinus ache, stomach ache and earache! I also had this constant nasty metallic taste in my mouth

On further investigation I found out the house had a problem with airbourne toxic black mould which can make some people very sick. In fact, the mould made me so ill I couldn't live in my new home.

N.B
✳ mould is a major cause of Sick Building Syndrome.

I couldn't believe it, Johnny couldn't believe it, <u>NO ONE</u> could believe it! I had to move out immediately and also get rid of all my possessions from the house. The mould specialist said if I took anything with m then I'd still have a reaction as my possessions woul have the mould spores on them. The next day I had to arrange for a house clearance company to take all my things away in a truck. Tears rolled down my face as I watched my <u>ENTIRE</u> life disappear before my eyes.

Wait! Come back!

Oh, Charlotte, I'm so sorry...

It was a desperately sad situation. Also, because Johnny Lucas had spent years building up his musical equipment it would have cost tens of thousands of pounds to replace it. I couldn't expect him to get rid of all his things too, and because we couldn't work out a solution, we started to get very stressed. The stress led to arguments and before we knew it we were constantly fighting. Eventually there was nothing left to do but split up. This was tragic as we both still loved each other, but we simply couldn't work out what else to do. Johnny then decided to move out to America to try his luck with his music out there, and I went to stay back at my brother's house in Notting Hill.

When he left I fell to the floor and sobbed. In fact, I sobbed for <u>six</u> <u>whole</u> <u>months</u>. I couldn't understand why life was so cruel.

Unsurprisingly, it wasn't long before the depression and anxiety reared their ugly heads again. I felt the gut-wrenching sadness and extreme panic almost as badly as I had the first time!

And then, after only a <u>month</u> of being in the states, Johnny suddenly got offered an amazing music deal out there!

Hooray!!! I've finally gone and made it! And in the states too!

When I heard the news I was distraught. I realised it'd mean Johnny would now live permanently in America – but the Shoeless Guru soon came to offer his wisdom on the matter.

I know you're sad but try to understand the mould was an incredible lesson. Firstly it has taught you not to be attached to material items, and secondly it's now teaching you about TRUE love... because if you love Johnny truly then you will want what's best for him, not what's best for you. Let him go and fulfil his destiny...

They were hard words to swallow but I knew in my heart the Shoeless Guru was right. So I picked myself up and tried as best I could to get on with life. When customers heard via the 'May The Thoughts Be With You' facebook page what had happened, they came to my stall to offer advice and support. Week after week countless people would appear. I was so touched by their kindness.

We've brought flowers, chocolates, teddy bears, tea and HUGS!

Oh my goodness! Everybody is being so lovely!

It took some months but by using the same tools I'd developed through my first bout of depression, I gradually did start to feel better again. And in that time I had also learnt how to love someone truly by being happy for Johnny that he was now happy elsewhere. Of course, I couldn't deny I still missed his company but the Professor of Truth soon solved that...!

Why don't you register on the Borrow My Doggy website and volunteer to look after someone's dog?! Dogs are excellent company and can have a positive impact on mental health - plus it will get you out and about and help keep you motivated.

What a fantastic idea, Professor! I'll do that!

It was the PERFECT solution. I'd look for a canine companion to spend my time with! As a child I'd always loved sausage dogs so I said a little prayer to ask for one to appear.

And as soon as I logged onto the website my prayers were answered. There, on the very first page, was a beautiful black and tan long-haired sausage dog named Bertie. I arranged to meet him and his owner in a local Notting Hill pub and when Bertie trotted through the door I knew instantly he was THE ONE!

I looked after Bertie 2 or 3 days every week while his owner was at work and, in fact, I still do to this day. He just comes to the market with me and takes great delight in lying snoozing under my stall all day!

Spending time around such a loving and affectionate animal really helped me get in touch with joy again. And I can safely say that now, a few years on, Bertie has helped me be the happiest I've been in a long, long time.

And that, dear reader, is the story so far. To this day Johnny Lucas is still in America having much success with his music, and I continue to sell my book at Portobello Market in Notting Hill. It's been an incredible journey with so many ups and downs but I wanted to share it as a message of hope to anyone going through a tough time. That's because when I was in the depths of my darkness I found it so comforting to read about other people who'd overcome difficulties. Simply hearing that they'd got beyond their adversities gave me faith that I could too. Their stories also gave me ideas for what might help me, as I hope my story will do for you.

Of course, everyone is different and what worked

for me may not be what works for you, but I hope you'll be inspired to keep going until you find a path to happy that _does_ suit you.

   This journey has also taught me that difficult life experiences often help us become the people we're truly capable of being – for example, if I hadn't gone through two years of depression and anxiety I wouldn't have got the material to write 'May The Thoughts Be With You'. If I hadn't developed the painful RSI I'd never have quit my job and become an author. If Johnny and I hadn't gone through the mould ordeal then he'd never have followed his dream to go to the States. And finally, if I didn't still, to this day, have to live with depersonalisation disorder I'd never have learnt how to accept something I cannot change, and find a way to be happy despite it.

I guess what I'm trying to say is that challenging experiences often lead us to a better life — and when they don't, they do at least always offer us the chance to become stronger, wiser and more compassionate. In short, we can learn from everything that happens, if we allow ourselves to. I hope that you've enjoyed this story and that it has helped in some small way. I also hope it's given you an insight

nto the world of mental ill health, and if you're
ruggling personally with a mental illness I hope you manage
o find a way to lead a fulfilling life, despite your
ondition, just as I have. I'll say good bye for now and
naybe see you at the stall one day! With much love,

Charlotte, Bertie
and all my
Characters ♡
x x x

photo credit: Renata Oliva

♥ Acknowledgements ♥

I wish there was enough space to mention everyone who's dear to me, but then this book would be twice the size! However, I do want to give special thanks to my mum and dad who are the loveliest parents I could have wished for. Thank you for my amazing upbringing, it was full of love, fun and endless help! Your consistency gave me such a good foundation that I felt brave enough to go out into the world and live my dreams. Thank you also for the times you run my market stall so I can have a weekend off! I also want to thank Kate and Rich from the bottom of my heart for your support in getting me through the worst period of my life. I wouldn't be who I am without you both, and that's why this book is, quite simply, for _you_!

Helpful Websites etc.

♥ www.acupuncture.org.uk

♥ www.brainbiocentre.com

♥ www.mind.org.uk

♥ www.samaritans.org

♥ www.survivingmold.com

♥ www.dpselfhelp.com (online forum for sufferers of depersonalisation disorder).

♥ Sufferers can also contact the Depersonalisation Disorder Service at the Maudsley Hospital, Camberwell, South London.